referencing

. . .

kate williams

For a complete listing of all **Palgrave Study Skills** titles, please visit:
www.palgrave.com/studyskills

contents

introduction

Referencing is a great invention! It enables researchers of all levels, from eminent professor to first year student, to show and share their research with their readers. Not convinced? Read on ...

First, you need to get your head around **what** referencing is, and **why** it is such an important aspect of writing at university. Once you have grasped this, **how** to reference becomes quite straightforward.

Part 1 starts with thinking about your research task and possible sources, and outlines how referencing works.

Part 2 considers the practical questions students often have about referencing.

Part 3 and **Part 4** are about **how** to reference, the main aim of the guide.

Part 3 gives a range of models and examples in the Harvard author-date style (the most widely used style) and Part 4 shows how numeric systems work with examples in the Vancouver (numeric) style often used in science subjects.

As you gain confidence in using the conventions of academic writing in your subject area you will develop confidence in your writing. Writing skills are only touched on here.

Many of the tips in this guide are developed in the Palgrave *Pocket Study Skills* series, in particular *Referencing and understanding plagiarism*. This series may be your next step for more detailed advice.

Specific links are suggested at the bottom of the page throughout this guide, and are referred to by their title. Full references for the linked books are given on p26 – of course!

Enjoy becoming a researcher.

referencing: the essentials

Referencing enables you to show your reading and research and how it has informed your thinking and understanding.

You have been set a task, have a reading list and are ready to go!

1 Choosing your sources

Before you start looking for sources to research your assignment or essay, you need to be clear about what exactly the task or question is asking you.

Different questions can be researched through different kinds of sources.

Books   journal articles   websites

are the essential sources of information, ideas and interpretation.

For practical advice on how to analyse the question, see *Planning your essay* Ch 4 and *Getting critical* Ch 10.
For a strategic approach to evaluating your sources, see *Getting critical* Ch 6.

You may, however, need to consult other types of sources current in your subject area and relevant to your task:

advertisements *Statistics*
Industry standards **company reports** photos
blogs newspapers or magazines **YouTube**
Leaflets Conference proceedings
Government reports or legislation
unpublished articles **theses or dissertations**

For any source, you have to decide if it is any good for your purpose.

Try using strategic questions as a checklist to help you evaluate the source and decide if you want to explore it further:

What?	How?
Why?	When?
Who?	Where?

Then ask the big question: **SO WHAT?**

- So … what are the implications? What do these answers tell me about the nature and quality of the source? Can I rely on it?
- So … is this source relevant to me and my purpose? How might it be useful to me?

Throughout your research, keep careful records, notes, and the full reference of every source you check out. You'll do a lot of work before you get anywhere near planning and writing your assignment or essay.

Your references are the record of your research. Look after them!

For tips on making effective notes, see *Reading and making notes* Parts 5 and 6.
For details on the stages of essay writing, see *Planning your essay* Ch 2.

2   Why reference?

The overarching reason why you need to reference is to show your reader where the **evidence** for what you say has come from. This will enable them to:

- go and check the source themselves (**traceability**)
- understand the nature, strengths and limitations, of your source (**authority** and **credibility**)
- form their own view about the source and the use you make of it (**reliability**).

The reader will also be able to see:

- the range of sources you have found and used, from textbooks to the reading list and beyond (**reach** and **scope**)
- your acknowledgement of the value of the efforts and findings of others (**politeness**).

3   How referencing works

There are many different referencing styles, and many more local variations. All operate on the same principles with two linked elements.

In your work you drop in a signal at the point in your writing where you use a source. This is a 'citation' that tells the reader two things:

- that the idea, point or evidence comes from your research
- where to look for more information about the source.

The signal is either

- a number in numeric systems[1] or (1) or [1] or
- the author + year of publication in (most) author-date systems.

In your reference list include ALL the sources you use, giving full details of where to find them. The list can be either in

- **number order** according to where you first use that source in your text (numeric style)

or
- **alphabetical order** by the author's last
  name (surname/family name) or name of the
  organisation (author-date style).

Whichever style you use, make sure
- every source you cite in your work is listed in your
  references section giving the details of where YOU
  found it
- every source listed in your references section is
  cited in your work.

4   Referencing styles

You will be asked to use a style from one of the
two 'families' below, or local adaptations of them.
Which style you use will depend on the conventions
and requirements of the subject area, and, to some
extent, on the preferences of your lecturers. Check
the style you are expected to use in each module you
take – it may vary.

Family 1: In-text name referencing styles

In your work cite the surname of the author(s) at
the point you draw on a source.

In your reference list give the full details of the
source so your reader can find it, in alphabetical
order, by surname of the first author:

In-text author/year of publication + Reference list

Harvard	APA
Widely used in: social science, business, health, science	(American Psychological Association) *Used in:* psychology

In-text author/page number + Reference list

MLA
(Modern Languages Association) *Used in:* some arts, humanities

A Harvard reference:

In your work
In developing countries too, overnutrition leads to malnutrition in children as well as undernutrition (Tzioumis and Adair 2014). Previously it had been thought …

In your reference list
Tzioumis E and Adair LS (2014). Childhood dual burden of under- and overnutrition in low- and middle-income countries: a critical review. *Food and Nutrition Bulletin*. 35(2) p230–243. Available at http://ingentaconnect.com [Accessed 21 March 2015]

For models and examples of references in Harvard style, see Part 3 of this guide.

Family 2: In-text numerical styles

In your work you use a number, in superscript[3] or brackets, round (3) or square [3] at the point where you draw on a source.

In your reference give the full details of the source and where to find it, in numbered order, with the first source you used listed as 1, the second as 2 and so on.

In-text number + Reference list in numerical order

Vancouver	IEEE
Widely used in: medicine, science, technology	*Used in*: some science, technology

For sample text and references in Vancouver style, see Part 4 of this guide.

In-text number + Footnotes

MHRA (Modern Humanities Research Association) *Used in*: some arts/ humanities.	OSCOLA *Used exclusively in* Law
Footnotes or **endnotes** are used both for references and for additional notes.	The full reference for each source is given in **footnotes.**
You may also be required to list all sources you used in a bibliography at the end.	You may be required to list secondary sources in a bibliography at the end.

A Vancouver reference:

In your work
In developing countries too, overnutrition leads to malnutrition in children as well as undernutrition[3]. Previously it had been thought …

In your reference list
3 Tzioumis E and Adair LS. Childhood dual burden of under- and overnutrition in low and middle income countries: a critical review. *Food and Nutrition Bulletin* 2014 June 35(2).

Read your course materials carefully to make sure you are clear about the style of referencing your tutor expects for that particular module or course. You may well be given guidance and helpful models to use. If so, do use them!

Your reading list may include not only essential and additional chapters and articles, but links to useful databases and websites. Take a hint! If these sources are suggested, make sure you check them out and use some of them.

Your references will show your research footprints, the record of your research. This in turn will form your knowledge base and shape your ideas.

referencing: FAQs

Part 2 is designed to offer quick guidance to some of the questions students often ask.

5 What style do I use?

Use the style your lecturer wants you to use!

Your course/module handbook should state which style to use. These may be specific to particular disciplines (such as MLA and MHRA in the arts; Vancouver in biomedicine/sciences; OSCOLA in law).

Harvard is the most used style across many disciplines, and within it, you'll find plenty of variations in house styles in the use of commas, full stops, italics, capitals and so on. They are all correct, though individual lecturers may have their preferences. Find a good model and use it consistently. Your course handbook, library or online guides are all good sources for models as well as this and other guides.

6 References or bibliography?

In Harvard a **reference list** is a list detailing all the sources you have actually consulted yourself and referred to in your writing.

Useful guides for style models include *Referencing and understanding plagiarism* and *Cite them right*.

A **bibliography** is a list of everything you have read in your research, whether you refer to it or not.

If you are asked for a bibliography for a finished piece of work, divide it into two sections:

1 *References* – for sources you cite in your text
2 *Other sources consulted* – for materials you have read but chose not to cite.

For subjects that use the term 'bibliography' instead of 'references' or 'reference list' see p6.

7 Your words or theirs?

Use your words in your writing. *Summarise* the idea or evidence you want to use from your reading, comment on it, and show how it relates to the point you are making.

Too much quoting: can give the impression that you do not understand the text you are drawing on and don't trust yourself to say anything about it.

Only quote words that are somehow special and be sure to comment on them.

Too much paraphrase: the same applies if you change a few words here and there, and put a name in brackets at the end (Williams 2015).

You are the writer. Your 'voice' needs to shine through.

8 Do I need page numbers?

If what you are referring to comes from a particular page, give the page number. So give the page number for a

• quote
• specific point, figure, diagram etc. that is contained on particular page(s).

The MLA style (used in some humanities subjects) uses page numbers in the text more extensively.

9   I found this source mentioned in a book ...

but you haven't actually read the source itself? The book you are reading is a **secondary** source, reporting on research or materials the authors have read and summarised in some way. These articles (data/reports/documents etc.) are the **primary**, first hand sources.

You don't list something in your references if you haven't actually read it. You list the text where YOU found it. This shows where you got it from and is enough to direct your reader to where they can find it.

In your work
The *Munro Review* of safeguarding and child protection argued for fundamental reform (Munro 2011, cited in Cooper, Gordon and Rixon 2014 p3).
Reference list
Cooper B, Gordon J and Rixon A (eds) (2014). *Best practice with children and families: Critical social work stories.* London: Palgrave.

10   The same author has several publications in the same year

Here your reader needs to know which publication (out of several) you are referring to where. This happens most often with

---

For advice on how to use your sources in your writing, See *Referencing and understanding plagiarism* Ch 6, *Writing for university* Ch 2, *Planning your dissertation* Part 6 and *Getting critical* Ch 12.

For more on primary and secondary sources and why they matter, see *Referencing and understanding plagiarism* and *Cite them right*.

- a government or official body that issues guidelines, policies or reports on a regular basis
- a weekly journalist who writes regularly on similar topics.

In your work
In order to achieve the six goals of *Education for All* at the national level in Egypt … (NCERD 2015c).
Reference list
NCERD (2015a) *Education for all 2015 national review: Cyprus.* Available at: www.unesco.org/new/en/education/themes/leading-the-international-agenda/education-for-all/resources/formulaires-unesdoc/ [Accessed 23 March 2015]
NCERD (2015b) *Education for all 2015 national review: Cuba.* Available at: www.unesco.org/new/en/education/themes/leading-the-international-agenda/education-for-all/resources/formulaires-unesdoc/ [Accessed 23 March 2015]
NCERD (2015c) *Education for all 2015 national review: Egypt.* Available at: www.unesco.org/new/en/education/themes/leading-the-international-agenda/education-for-all/resources/formulaires-unesdoc/ [Accessed 23 March 2015]

11   Should I use a reference manager?

You may find a reference manager helpful for a longer piece of work like a dissertation, so it is a good idea familiarise yourself with more than one and decide. University libraries will have some available free to students (like Endnote). Others are free to any user.

It is easy to find a comparison of various types of reference management software by searching online.

using Harvard (author-date) style: models and examples

12 How to reference a book

The six points of a book reference

1 **Author**(s) or **editor**(s) as shown on the title page: family name/surname first, followed by initial(s)
2 **Year** of publication (in brackets).
   Give the date of the edition you are using
3 **Title** of the book in *italics*
4 **Edition** (if not first)
5 **Place** of publication (city/town/state/country)
6 **Publisher**

Book references

One author: In your work
As Rassool (2014) points out, in today's diverse patient community …
Reference list
Rassool GH (ed) (2014). *Cultural competence in caring for Muslim patients*. Basingstoke: Palgrave Macmillan.

Two or three authors: In your work
Cooper, Gordon and Rixon (2014) imply that …
Reference list
Cooper B, Gordon J and Rixon A (eds) (2014). *Best practice with children and families: Critical social work stories.* London: Palgrave.

Four or more authors: In your work
Strategies can be categorised according to … (Jolibert et al. 2012)
Reference list
Jolibert A, Mühlbacher H, Flores L and Dubois PL (2012). *Marketing management: A value-creation process* (2nd edition). Basingstoke: Palgrave Macmillan.

A chapter in an edited book

In your work
In your writing, you refer to author(s) of the chapter you are using. Your reader looks for that name in your references.
Lovering (2014 p30) suggests that nurses …
Reference list
The name of the author(s) of the chapter leads you to the book it is in.
Lovering S (2014). Caring as an act of spirituality: A nursing approach. In Rassool GH (ed), *Cultural competence in caring for Muslim patients* (2nd edition). Basingstoke: Palgrave Macmillan. pp27–38.

eBooks

When an eBook looks like a printed book, and has all the details of a printed book, reference it like a printed book.

If the eBook does not have the format or details of a printed book on your device, use the information you do have. For example:

In your work
This behaviour can be compared to … (Wynne and Udell 2013).
Reference list
Wynne C and Udell M (2013). *Animal cognition: Evolution, behaviour and cognition* (2nd edition). CourseSmart. Available at: http://www.coursesmart.com/animal-cognition-2nd-edition/clive-d-l-wynne-monique-a-r-udell/dp/9781137367297 [Accessed 17 March 2015].

13   How to reference a journal article

The six points of a journal reference
1 **Author**(s) in the order shown: family name/surname first, followed by initial(s) 2 **Year** of publication (in brackets) 3 Full **title of article** 4 **Title of journal** in *italics* 5 **Details:** Volume / issue / month (where given) 6 **Pages** of the article

These are the details you use for a hard copy journal on a library shelf. Academic databases are the new library shelf – the location is fixed and they don't move around like other online sources.

Increasingly articles are located via their doi (Digital Object Identifier) typed into a search engine. Electronic journal articles and the electronic version of printed articles can be referred to by their doi. If you include the doi, the details of Available at … / Accessed … are not relevant or needed.

However, many journals do not use the doi for articles (such as the one on p5), and lecturers may still want to see Available at … / Accessed: for all journal article references. Where this is the case, include them! Both ways of showing the location of an article are valid.

Journal article references

One author: In your work

… whereas multiparty coalition governments are more likely to … (Colomer 2012).

Reference list

Colomer J (2012). The more parties, the greater policy stability. *European Political Science.* 11(2) pp229–243. Available at: www.palgrave-journals.com [Accessed 17 March 2015]

Two or three authors: In your work

Bullock and Tilley (2008) stress that this problem should not …

Reference list

Bullock K and Tilley N (2008). Understanding and tackling gang violence. *Crime Prevention and Community Safety.* 10(1) pp36–47. doi: 10.1057/palgrave.cpcs.8150057

Four or more authors: In your work

Public health policy should address wider issues that affect educational outcomes … (Siddiqi et al. 2011). In areas that …

Reference list

Siddiqi A, Kawachi I, Berkman L, Hertzman C and Subramanian S V (2011). Education determines a nation's health, but what determines educational outcomes? A cross-national comparative analysis. *Journal of Public Health Policy.* 33(1) pp1–15. Available at: http://www.palgrave-journals.com/jphp/journal/v33/n1/full/jphp201152a.html [Accessed 17 March 2015]

14 How to reference a webpage/ internet source

The five points of a webpage reference
1 **Author**, individual(s) or organisation
2 **Year** the site or page was written or updated
3 **Title** of the webpage *in italics*
4 **Available at**: url
5 **Accessed**: date you accessed it

In your work
According to WWF (2015) a quarter of a million turtles die each year in fishing lines. WWF argue that a small …
Reference list
WWF (2015). *Help us save marine turtles*. Available at: https://support.wwf.org.uk/save-the-turtle [Accessed 19 March 2015]

You can of course reference any webpage:

In your work
As the best communicators in a business, PR professionals have the ability to become CEOs (Rajan 2015).
Reference list
Rajan M (2015). *Why PR needs a seat at the leadership table*. Available at: https://www.linkedin.com/pulse/why-pr-needs-seat-leadership-table-mukund-rajan?trk=tod-posts-post1-ptlt [Accessed 19 March 2015]

This website has the full details, but can you rely on it?

This is where your critical awareness kicks in. Just because you find the nugget of information you were looking for, it doesn't mean that this is a sensible source to use. Check it out carefully. Your

For how to evaluate sources, see *Getting critical* Ch 6.

assignment or your argument is only as good as the evidence on which it is based.

If you do decide to use it, you need to cite it as fully as possible. Where details are missing include the remaining details:

No date

In your work
As the best communicators in a business, PR professionals have the ability to become CEOs (Rajan no date).
Reference list
Rajan M (no date). *Why PR needs a seat at the leadership table*. Available at: https://www.linkedin.com/pulse/why-pr-needs-seat-leadership-table-mukund-rajan?trk=tod-posts-post1-ptlt [Accessed 19 March 2015]

No author

In your work
As the best communicators in a business, PR professionals have the ability to become CEOs (*Why PR needs a seat at the leadership table* 2015).
Reference list
Why PR needs a seat at the leadership table (2015). Available at: https://www.linkedin.com/pulse/why-pr-needs-seat-leadership-table-mukund-rajan?trk=tod-posts-post1-ptlt [Accessed 19 March 2015]

No author or title

In your work
As the best communicators in a business, PR professionals have the ability to become CEOs (https://www.linkedin.com/pulse/why-pr-needs-seat-leadership-table-mukund-rajan?trk=tod-posts-post1-ptlt 2015).

Reference list
https://www.linkedin.com/pulse/why-pr-needs-seat-leadership-table-mukund-rajan?trk=tod-posts-post1-ptlt (2015) [Accessed 19 March 2015]

The less you know about a website, the less you should *rely* on it or use it as evidence in your writing. If you are using it as a primary source, however – for example, in a discussion about language used in online communication, or marketing tools – it could be a useful source to refer to.

You have no way of knowing if unidentifiable webpages floating in cyberspace are credible or reliable sources of evidence – except by using your own common sense and critical questioning.

15 Guidelines for referencing other sources

You will by now have identified a broad pattern to the information you record and cite for any source you use. Typically this includes:

- **Author:** (person(s) or organisation)
- **Year** of publication
- **Title** of item (e.g. webpage, image, post, newspaper, magazine, TV, film) in *italics*
- **Title** of 'host' (website, publication, organisation, publisher, convenor)
- **Helpful details** to locate it including url
- **Date** you accessed it

Beyond this, look for a model closest to the item you want to reference and adapt it, presenting the details you have. Be transparent about what your source is, and be helpful to your reader so they can track it down.

Below are some examples of other sources often used by students.

Newspapers and magazines

In your work
… but it appears that the Amazon is an exception to this trend (Mathiesen 2015).
Reference list
Mathiesen K (2015). Amazon's trees removed nearly a third less carbon in last decade – study. *The Guardian*. Available at: http://www.theguardian.com/environment/2015/mar/18/amazons-trees-remove-third-less-carbon-decade-ago-emissions [Accessed 19 March 2015].

Brochures and leaflets

In your work
Sport England (2013) claims that political interest in sport has never been higher.
Reference list
Sport England (2013). *Want to make a difference to community sport?* London: Sport England.

For examples of even more sources, see *Cite them right*.

Reports and company documentation

In your work
The supermarket Tesco recognises that the internet and social media have impacted on footfall … (Tesco PLC 2014).
Reference list
Tesco PLC (2014). *Annual report and financial statements 2014*. Cheshunt: Tesco PLC. Available at: http://www.tescoplc.com/files/pdf/reports/ar14/download_strategic_report.pdf [Accessed 19 March 2015].

Statistics

In your work
In quarter 3 in 2014 visits abroad increased by over 2% … (Office for National Statistics 2014).
Reference list
Office for National Statistics (2014). *Overseas travel and tourism – quarterly release, Q3 2014*. Available at: www.ons.gov.uk/ons/rel/ott/overseas-travel-and-tourism---quarterly-release/q3–2014/index.html [Accessed 23 March 2015].

Research report

In your work
UNHCR (2015 p11) points out that while the number of refugees increased, the downward trend in those returning to their countries continued …
Reference list
UNHCR (2015). *UNHCR Mid-year trends 2014*. Geneva: UNHCR. Available at: http://unhcr.org/54aa91d89.html [Accessed 19 March 2015].

TV and radio

In your work
Worshippers were said to have been thrown … (BBC News 2015).
Reference list
BBC News (2015). BBC1. 20 March 2015.

Film/video/YouTube

In your work
In *October Event 2014* (2014), Phil Schiller introduces …
Reference list
Apple (2014). *October Event 2014*. Available at: https://www.youtube.com/watch?v=sBfvJn-fpnc [Accessed 19 March 2015].

Photos and images

In your work
Early photos of the star, such as *Tracy and Hepburn in Woman of The Year* (Cukor 1942) …
Reference list
Cukor G (1942). *Tracy and Hepburn in Woman of the Year*. Available at: http://www.corbisimages.com/stock-photo/rights-managed/42–17363213/tracy-and-hepburn-in-woman-of-the?popup=1 [Accessed 19 March 2015].

Social media

In your work
Apple is negotiating with broadcasters to stream many of the big television networks straight to Apple TV (Metz 2015).

Reference list
Metz C (2015). People might actually buy the new Apple TV. *Wired*. Business. March 23 07:00. Available at: http://www.wired.com/2015/03/people-might-actually-buy-new-apple-tv/ [Accessed 23 March 2015].

4

using Vancouver (numeric) style: text and examples

This section shows how a numeric referencing style works. This style is most commonly used in science, medicine and related subjects. It focuses the reader's attention on the research, which is fully referenced in the 'references' section at the end. It is also economical with the word count!

In your work
• Use a number in superscript[3] or brackets, round (3) or square [3] at the point where you draw on a source to make the link with the full reference in your reference list.
• The first source you refer to is (1) and so on.
• You can use the same number to refer to the same source again.
• You can refer to more than one source if you are using them to support the same point.[13 14]

Reference list
• References are listed in the order you draw on them in your text, starting with[1] or (1); author's surname first (person or organisation).
• The year goes at the end of the reference, before the page numbers or URL (where used).
• The title of the book or journal (or 'host') is in italics. Journal titles are sometimes abbreviated.
• There is some variation in how many author names you list before putting 'et al.'. Six authors is a reasonable cut-off point.

The text below shows how this works with a specially written but realistic example of good student writing on exercise and health. The full references of all the sources referred to in the text are listed in number order in the 'References'. In this example each type of source is identified in the tag above it.

You would not do this in your work!

The sample text and references in Vancouver style has been researched and devised by Victoria Coathup, with thanks.

Regular aerobic exercise has been shown to reduce the risk of developing a number of chronic conditions, including cardiovascular disease, type 2 diabetes[1], hypertension, obesity, osteoporosis, and certain types of cancer[2]; it has also been suggested as an effective method of dealing with the symptoms of depression and anxiety[3].

The current UK guidelines recommend adults to participate in at least 150 minutes of moderate-intensity aerobic activity, such as cycling or fast walking, every week, and muscle-strengthening activities on 2 or more days a week that work all major muscle groups[4].

A government report published in 2012 found that 33% of men and 45% of women, over the age of 16, did not meet these recommendations for aerobic exercise[5]. A wide variety of techniques have been assessed in health care interventions, in a bid to increase physical activity levels in adult populations; ranging from cognitive based therapies[6] to community support[7].

References

Book chapter

1   Praet SFE, Rozenburg R, Van Loon L JC. Type
    2 diabetes. In: Saxton J. M. (ed) *Exercise and
    Chronic Disease, an evidence based approach*.
    Oxon: Routledge. 2011.

Book (print)

2   Kenny WL, Wilmore JH, Costill DL. *Physiology
    of Sport and Exercise*. 5th edition. Champaign,
    Illinois: Human Kinetics. 2012.

Journal article (print)

3   Lawlor DA, Hopker SW. The effectiveness of
    exercise as an intervention in the management
    of depression: systematic review and meta-
    regression analysis of randomized controlled trials.
    BMJ. 2011; 322(7289): 763–767.

Website

4   NHS. *Physical activity guidelines for adults*
    [online]. NHS choices. 2013. Available from:
    http://www.nhs.uk/livewell/fitness/pages/physical-
    activity-guidelines-for-adults.aspx [Accessed 23rd
    March 2015].

Government report

5   Health and Social Care Information Centre.
    *Statistics on Obesity, Physical Activity and Diet:
    England 2014*. ONS. 2014.

**Conference proceedings
(individual paper)**

6   French DP, Olander EK. Which behavior change
    techniques are most effective at increasing older
    adults self-efficacy and physical activity. In: The
    British Psychological Society. *Division of Health
    Psychology Annual Conference*. Brighton: The
    British Psychological Society; 2013.

| Journal article (electronic) |

7   Baker PR, Francis DP, Soares J, Weightman AL, Foster C. Community wide interventions for increasing physical activity. Cochrane Database of Systematic Reviews. 2015. (1). DOI: 10.1002/14651858.CD008366.pub3 [Accessed 23rd March 2015].

And finally ... becoming a researcher

Being able to reference with confidence will go a long way towards making you a confident and competent researcher. To reference well you do need the technical skill of setting out references correctly in your work and in your references list. I hope this guide has helped with this.

Referencing with confidence will also enable you to become a researcher yourself. You acknowledge the contribution each source makes to your knowledge and understanding of the subject matter, and debates in your subject area.

Enjoy!

Linked books in the *Palgrave Study Skills* and *Pocket Study Skills* series

Cottrell S (2013). *The study skills handbook* (4th edition). Basingstoke: Palgrave Macmillan.

Godfrey J (2013). *How to use your reading in your essays* (2nd edition). Basingstoke: Palgrave Macmillan.

Godfrey J (2014). *Reading and making notes* (2nd edition). Basingstoke: Palgrave Macmillan.

Godfrey J (2011). *Writing for university*. Basingstoke: Palgrave Macmillan.

Godwin J (2014). *Planning your essay* (2nd edition). Basingstoke: Palgrave Macmillan.

Pears R and Shields G (2013). *Cite them right*. Basingstoke: Palgrave Macmillan.

Williams K (2014). *Getting critical* (2nd edition). Basingstoke: Palgrave Macmillan.

Williams K (2013). *Planning your dissertation*. Basingstoke: Palgrave Macmillan.

Williams K and Carroll J (2009). *Referencing and understanding plagiarism*. Basingstoke: Palgrave Macmillan.